The Gender Spectrum

A Compendium of All the Known Genders

That kid from Kindergarten Cop

ISBN-10: 1548962481
ISBN-13: 978-1548962487

DEDICATION

To all who have watched the world slowly descend into chaos and wondered if there would ever be a definitive reassertion of practical reality into the public discourse, I humbly provide this compilation.

CONTENTS

CHAPTER 1

BOYS

Boys have a penis.

CHAPTER 2

GIRLS

Girls have a vagina.

The end.

That kid from Kindergarten Cop

Appendix:

A continued discussion on the topic…

Because Amazon wouldn't publish my book with 90 more empty pages. I decided to include some of the more interesting exchanges I've had with the "True Believers" (TB). The names of the True Believers have been changed to protect their identities. Timelines have also been removed.

I don't claim to be some brilliant debate and rhetoric expert. If you want that, I suggest listening to some of the things that Dr. Jordan Peterson, Ben Shapiro, and others have said on this topic. I just make my little jokes and sometimes people respond with their side, of course their side is ridiculous but they feel passionate enough about it to humor my penchant for being argumentative. I enjoy the discussion even when it gets a bit sideways and insults happen (fair warning, I'm not above trading those, and you will see them), but I do like to stick to the subject whenever possible. So enjoy the appendix.

<u>A bit about TB1: He is one of the Q in the never-ending acronym. He's "questioning" not fully committed to anything except making the argument for what he feels himself leaning toward. He enjoys the debate and is capable of the mental gymnastics necessary to maintain his position without just surrendering outright. So enjoy my exchange with TB1.</u>

<u>TB1 to That kid from Kindergarten Cop</u>

You and I had a debate last week and because you wrote in detail where you were coming from (which I appreciate), I grasped what you were getting at.

Unfortunately, your issue with trans people is only comparable to an example you gave about claiming to be Chinese when you are Caucasian. The stuff about Assad, Kim Jong Un, CEOs, Kanye West don't apply, they are apples to oranges.

People who transition, like Jenner, know what their DNA is. Everyone knows what their DNA and chromosomes are. Due to the pressure to communicate efficiently, the details of trans issues get lost in the one/two page internet articles and five minute t.v. clips, most of which are written/spoken by people with very little grasp of the realities of anything trans.

What Jenner is saying is "I identify as female, and have changed my body to get as close to being physical female as possible. I know I am genetically male."

So she's not saying she is "Chinese" when actually "Caucasian". She's saying she prefers to be Chinese and has taken the steps she thinks she needs to take to be content, while knowing that, yes, she's Caucasian genetically.

However, the above won't fly in media discussions, it's too boring and too detailed, even though it's far more reflective of reality.

Disagreeing with Jenner or anyone who transitions or anyone gender variant is one thing. However, your movie quote is a simplification. Seems to me it is a reaction to the simplification of identity issues that is going on publicly.

That kid from Kindergarten Cop to TB1

I have no doubt that there are people who truly believe that they are the opposite sex. But here's another gaping hole in that theory:

You cannot possibly know what it means to be the opposite sex.

Your displeasure with your genetics is not a reasonable position. You might as well walk outside and complain that the clouds are in the wrong place, the trees are the wrong species, and the temperature is all wrong.

There are things beyond your control, the circumstances of your birth is just one of those things. What you are doing when you claim to "identify" as something you are not is reducing what you observe to be the entirety of the other's being. You, if you are a male, cannot possibly identify with what it was like to have your first period during 3rd period English. You are many times less likely to have been perved on by a male relative. You can't know what it was like to go bra shopping the first time with your mother. The list is practically endless. If you are a female, you have never been kicked in the testicles. You didn't have to hide your erection while moving from class to class. You have likely never been hit in the face by the biggest guy in the school or felt any pressure to play violent sports by your peers whether it appealed to you or not. Same endless list of sex specific experiences applies. Are they comparable, sure, but your ability to empathize and fantasize do not qualify as your admission ticket to the club. Now who has been over simplifying things?

TB1 to That kid from Kindergarten Cop

I don't think we are debating the same things. Physiology isn't in dispute with me and it never has been. I want to discover the nature of identity. As a psychology grad, surely you have read a lot about the nature of the psyche and perceptions of self. If it was simple, there wouldn't be thousands of books full of theories about it, nor would our understanding of it be constantly evolving.

Are identities automatic due to physiology? There are no influences from family, culture, personal choice? If so, then best be having a chat with anyone you know who is Christian and feels Jesus is with them, because there's no biological basis for that. If Christians in the West grew up in India, most would be Hindu, with no connection to the spirit of Jesus.

Experiences due to physiology, like (most of) the ones you give above, can lead to being able to relate to people who have the been through the same things ... but it doesn't automatically make you feel like one of the broader category of 'man' or 'woman'.

Perhaps your opposition comes from seeing the government change birth certificates, etc. Personally, I don't believe birth certificates should have sex designations on them anyway. And they are historical documents, I am uncomfortable changing them retroactively.

So it looks like people like Jenner are directly disputing DNA. But it ain't that simple. The way the system for legal identification is set up, people who transition can't get other I.D. without legally changing their birth certificate. If that wasn't a requirement (why does sex designation need to be on a driver's license?) then perhaps it wouldn't be necessary.

That kid from Kindergarten Cop to TB1

The nature of identity should at least be natural. Your perception of yourself should be based on your previous experiences, an honest assessment of your current state, and a goal for your personal development in the future. Your previous experiences should serve as a guide to your future development. If you have been a video game nerd for the first 25 years of your life and tip the scales at 3 bills, it's probably not realistic to expect that you will become a world class mountain climber. If you just got out of prison for armed robbery it is not realistic to expect to be an ivy league educated brain surgeon. If you are a professional MMA fighter and lose your sight, you can probably give up on being the champ. If you are born with a penis you will never be a mother. Of all of these scenarios only one of them is 100% impossible.

How you feel about your spiritual life is your own feelings similar to your identity. You can yell in my face "the power of Christ compels you" until you pass out but if I don't agree, I'm not compelled. If you tell me that Christ is standing right next to me and I am clearly alone then I have just as much problem with that as I do with you claiming to be a gender inconsistent with your biology.

If the experiences I listed do not make you feel like part of the broader category of "man" or "woman", how does their rejection gain your greater feeling a part of the opposite sex? While you are entitled to reject the life experiences that you share with half the world, you still will never know the experiences of the other half.

My opposition has nothing to do with the government. Government is a group of people, way too numerous, far too lazy, and generally unconcerned with making the world better. You want a birth certificate with a different name? No problem. Different sex? No problem. Since they don't affect money, you can be whatever you want. They really don't care. If they are going to issue documentation however, it should be accurate and including all of the identifying measures, including gender, seems like a fair baseline. But honestly, if the political arm of your insane movement is looking for a "W" to go on the scoreboard, you could have that removed in California before the end of the year, I'd put money on it.

Why does sex designation need to be on a driver's license? Same reason eye color, height, weight, and DOB are, it is part of your identity.

TB1 to That kid from Kindergarten Cop

Video game nerd = choice. Getting to three bills = choice plays a role. Robbery = choice. Brain surgeon = choice. MMA fighter = choice. Losing sight = bad luck.

Five of those six are choices.

No one can influence the circumstances of their birth. You want to automatically confer an identity on a person because of something where there is no choice ... yet every comparison you give involves at least one choice, most involve two.

And driver's licenses don't include ethnicity - isn't part of your identity too?

That kid from Kindergarten Cop to TB1

Previous experiences and an honest assessment of your current state. What previous experience do you have as the opposite sex that would lead you to believe that you have future potential with that group? What honest assessment of your current state leads you to believe that you can be something that you lack the basic equipment to qualify as? If you took the radical action of surgery to mimic what you can't possibly understand, what about the end product would bring you joy? Living a lie in physical form is much worse than the confusion and discomfort you have now.

Being a video game nerd, an armed robber, a brain surgeon, or MMA fighter are choices, but also parts of people's identity. They are roles that people play and they invite certain presumptions based on those identifying roles. You have mental images of these people in your mind already, those are the presumptions that people who assume those identities assume. They, or others, would tell you that they are these things if they were asked to describe themselves or be described. You cannot practice hard, gamble your freedom, study, or train to be the opposite sex, you can only believe it and mutilate your body, but you are still subject to others opinions on the matter. You asked for a discussion about identity. There's one.

I'm not opposed to mentioning ethnicity on a DL if you can clearly determine it, but unlike the gender binary that defines 99.9+% of people, race and ethnicity truly can be a spectrum so that becomes legitimately messy, unlike gender.

TB1 to That kid from Kindergarten Cop

Jesus, guy. You are more intense about this than I am, and you aren't trans/gender-variant.

What gives? Why do you care so much what other adults do, provided they don't harm others?

That kid from Kindergarten Cop to TB1

If it were only other adults and it truly did not harm others, you would have an argument, but adults are pressuring other adults to buy into or demand that others tolerate the ridiculous notion that being "trans" or "gender-variant" is something other than mental illness. Your push to redefine your depression as something new, an over-arching "identity" that is somehow immune from inputs from the rest of the world, is hurting people who will now channel all of their hope for escape from the tyranny of their minds into a surgery that can radically alter their physical self but does not address where the true problem lies.

And all of this pressure is harming children. Giving children the false idea that surgery and hormones will make everything better is cruel. Even the truly single minded child who wants to be the other sex does not want to be a chemically dependent, inconsistent, and invalid mimic version of what they want to be, it will forever remain a fantasy. When that child reaches the developmental milestones and cannot identify with anyone at all, they can't find solace in their peers shared experiences, do you think that depression will subside or compound? When the child rejects their peers because the child believes themselves to be different, that's one thing. When the child is rejected by his peers because his peers know that they are different, that has to be worse.

All of the above is just on an interpersonal level and has nothing to do with all of the legal and societal bovine excrement that our lazy government has unleashed by licensing this insanity.

TB1 to That kid from Kindergarten Cop

1) I specifically said adults for a reason. The debate is different for children and teenagers.

2) You said the government had nothing to do with your opposition. Looks like it does.

3) Did you transition and regret it or something? Or someone you know transition and regret it?

That kid from Kindergarten Cop to TB1

Adults are the parents of these children. This kind of perverse thinking is being projected onto children by parents who are buying into your line of bull that being "gender-variant" is something other than insane. It's just sickening to watch.

I am not mad at the government. How can I be? I expected

nothing else. I told you that they are lazy and will give you whatever you want if you just pay the fee. The fact that they are lazy has led to the downstream societal destruction that results in grown men being legally allowed to go into the ladies room or lockers with my wife and daughter based on nothing more than his state of mind. That is the goal of this culturally Marxist tactic, to cause chaos. I do believe that the government was behind the movement with Obama at the helm, but now has corrected course. But ultimately, without an outside influence, government will screw it up one way or another. I could no more be mad about the government screwing it up than I could be mad that Charlie Sheen drinks and does coke, it is a defining characteristic, an identity, you could say.

I don't know anyone, personally, who has expressed any interest in your insane position. I do have a cousin who struggles to project her femininity based on the fact that she is 6'1" and probably around 200 sturdy, not terribly distributed, pounds. Her whole family is large, her three brothers are 6'3" or taller and 250 at the lightest. She is very sweet and modest but I would not want to be on her bad side. I know her struggle is different but she, even if she wanted to, could never be a man. Bigger than the average, stronger than the average, but still not a man.

I understand that people struggle with their place, role, identity in this world, but demanding special rights, threatening self-harm, and calling everyone else who insists on reality a "bigot" for not recognizing your status as a special snowflake is too much to bear. That's why I make it a point to engage with those that would attempt to argue your position and reaffirm that what you are after will not come about unless the world fell apart due to the lack of anyone being able to discuss any version of truth in the world.

TB1 to That kid from Kindergarten Cop

I'm Libertarian/Conservative. You can't possibly think every single person who supports trans rights is a progressive. So kindly respond to what I'm writing and don't bring in your negative feelings towards the snowflakes. I don't like their shrieking dramatics, even though I occasionally agree with their viewpoint on an issue.

Children should not take hormones or have surgery. I support adults' rights to do so. Bodily autonomy is vital for individual freedom. Adults can do what they wish as long as others aren't harmed. Whether or not they should is up to them. I've known several trans people who have taken hormones/undergone surgery and they are productive, law abiding contributing members of society, and they seem to varying degrees to be satisfied with their decision.

The world isn't going to fall apart, that's just histrionics. Disagree all you want, it's vital for all issues that people speak their mind. But the drama on display is the conservative version of needing a safe space.

And I don't think you are a terrible person for holding your viewpoints. The word 'bigot' is tossed around way too much these days.

Perhaps you could google 'gender-variant', by the way, before insisting it's a perverted mental illness. I prefer being gender variant. If I had a choice, it's what I'd pick. And I've been at this over half my life (20+) years.

That kid from Kindergarten Cop to TB1

The libertarian angle is not completely objectionable but it still perpetuates the lie. In a vacuum, that philosophy is fine, but like I said, the entire concept is a lie and cannot be shielded from children any more than their parents sex lives, drug use, or other vices.

If you are a male who presents as a female you are perpetrating a falsehood, misrepresenting your true self. It lures real females into a false sense of familiarity and security and claims unearned female privilege from other males. If you are a female who presents as male, you claim untrue male privilege and invite challenges you are unprepared to meet. It is equally deceptive and violates common decency. Those who might know of your ongoing deception and do not tell others, participate in making a fool of others, it is impolite, at best. You can't truly wonder why you might be disliked.

High functioning insane people are nothing new. How many serial killers were considered productive, law abiding (otherwise) members of society before they were discovered? Obviously trannies =/= serial killers in offense to society but again, high functioning mental cases are not unusual.

The world falling apart is the only way to remove such a foundational, simple, and vitally important distinction from society. If assumptions so basic as who to ask to open a jar of pickles can't be made, what are we doing? If we are in the woods and a bathroom break is needed but "Robert" is really "Roberta" what does she do on the tree? What about the guy who just wants to be courteous and not show his junk to a lady, regardless of how she's dressed or feeling that day? You've robbed him of his ability to work within the confines of his conscience by deceiving him, that's how we want to treat people? The social fabric of a civil society requires a certain baseline understanding of proper interaction and lying about something so basic undermines that baseline, it is chaos. It could not be more destructive to society. It is a cancer to civilizations.

Gender variant, gender non conforming, whatever. If you're a sissy boy, that's fine. If you are a tomboy or bull LPGA pro, that's also fine (hell, you could have been POTUS and the first lady for the last 8 years). But you can never be the opposite sex. And, for what it's worth, your level or length of disturbance is of no consequence to the discussion. You'll find nothing beyond sympathy for your mental anguish. It does not make an argument.

TB1 to That kid from Kindergarten Cop

Serial killers - gonna need a new Godwin's law for that one. You lose the minute you mention them.

In case you were not aware of it, serial killers by definition are not law abiding.

It should not be this easy to refute your arguments. You seem too perceptive. But you don't have any experiences is this area, so 99% of your thoughts are limited to theory only. This is how progressive academics come to their conclusions.

Maybe time for a new career?

That kid from Kindergarten Cop to TB1

So then you can't argue against the point that there are indeed high functioning insane people, so instead, you try invoke Godwin's law? I did include the caveat "otherwise" on "law abiding", in case you missed it. That hardly refutes any argument.

Anyone who has ever been the butt of a joke or deceived in any way should be angered by someone who is attempting a deception. I tell my children that nothing makes me angrier than being lied to. It is not just that they are concealing the truth, it is a gamble and assertion that they are the smarter party in exchange, it is disrespectful and offensive. And if you enable it in others, you are just as offensive.

TB1 to That kid from Kindergarten Cop

Of course it refutes an argument. You went for a preposterous comparison that wasn't even close to being legitimate. Law abiding refers to 'actually law abiding', not 'giving the appearance of law abiding' or 'otherwise law abiding'.

Serial killers are 'Hail Mary' passes in debating. Only someone with little understanding of an issue would reference them unless the debate was specifically about serial killers.

That kid from Kindergarten Cop to TB1

One more time, the larger point was "high functioning insane people". Many serial killers are high functioning, many trannies are high functioning, that is the analogy to show that trannies are not unique in their ability to function within society at a high level, while still displaying behaviors far outside the "norm". Here's another one, kleptomaniacs are, many times, high functioning and successful people, who feel compelled to commit antisocial behavior (theft). White collar embezzling bankers play by the rules and function at high enough levels to gain control of the levers of financial power before revealing they will commit antisocial behavior (financial fraud). Murder, theft, and financial fraud are all illegal, both malum in se, and malum prohibitum, but though it may not be codified in law, interpersonal fraud (lying) is malum in se and part of each of these other criminals' repertoire. Does your extension of Godwin's law apply to kleptomaniacs, and embezzlers, too? I think it is safe to say that you were just looking for an "out" because you couldn't refute the point that trannies being high functioning does not make the world forget that they are still committing antisocial behaviors by committing interpersonal fraud.

TB1 to That kid from Kindergarten Cop

Hey look! It's the guy who can't provide an opinion that isn't easily refutable.

You came close once, I'll give you that.

That kid from Kindergarten Cop to TB1

So refute "Boys have a penis. Girls have a vagina". Go ahead.

TB1 to That kid from Kindergarten Cop

Physical males have a penis. Physical females have a vagina.

Don't mix up objective biology with subjective identity of "boy" or "girl" and viola! Issue solved. Just because identity and dna match what is expected for most people does not mean they have to match for everyone.

That kid from Kindergarten Cop to TB1

Yes, we know, some people are bat guano crazy and think their "subjective identity" means something to other people. That's insane.

TB1 to That kid from Kindergarten Cop

Come on, man. At least I put real thought into my opinion to go along with the insult. You are just doing the insult. Makes me think you know I am right.

That kid from Kindergarten Cop to TB1

Fine, let me ask you this then, if you immediately capitulate and accept that you, and everybody else, have to treat these crazy people according to how they feel that day, what won't you go along with? If objective reality is to take a back seat to the subjective experience of another in your mind, you are easier to manipulate than warm play dough. If you would stand on the feelings of an obviously confused snowflake and take up the fight against objective reality, you are a useful idiot for the insane.

TB1 to That kid from Kindergarten Cop

I am able to balance objective reality with my own subjectivity. Someone telling me how they identify does not alter my belief about their dna. And I have never had anyone who transitioned try and tell me b.s. about their biology. They know what their dna is.

You are asking them to go along with your subjective belief about who they are just as much as they are doing it to you. Don't agree with them? You don't have to. But stop telling them they have to agree with you.

That kid from Kindergarten Cop to TB1

My belief is not "subjective", it is based on reality, biological reality. Reality that is empirical to the disinterested observer is the arbiter of the truth. Individuals such as Bruce Jenner, Riley Dennis, and others who are nowhere near to "passing" would, by anyone unfamiliar with their protestations to the contrary, be determined to be men. That is the standard that the rest of the world adheres to and the only standard that makes any sense.

Trannies don't have to agree with me, I am not putting forth an opinion that would be validated by agreement from anyone, I am simply stating fact. I would not force anyone to behave in a manner consistent with reality if they are insane, but I would also not behave, myself, in a manner inconsistent with reality just to humor an insane person. Two wrongs don't make a right.

TB1 to That kid from Kindergarten Cop

All beliefs are subjective. DNA is not, it is objective. No one disputes that.

What is being argued about is whether dna determines identity.

That kid from Kindergarten Cop to TB1

Yes, of course, DNA determines identity!

It can send you to death row or be your ticket off of it. That, life and death, is one of the starkest difference you can make.

DNA IS IDENTITY!

Will I have to pick my mic up off the floor to further destroy your already obliterated attempt at making a logical argument?

TB1 to That kid from Kindergarten Cop

Uh oh. We got ourselves a mic dropper!

Dude, dna influences identity. If you think it is the only influence then you don't have much appreciation for the experience of being human.

May I suggest you do some travelling?

That kid from Kindergarten Cop to TB1

DNA is not destiny but it is identity, it is the characteristic measure of scientific and legal definitions of identity. If Bruce Jenner had split the scene of his vehicular manslaughter incident and the CSI team found his cigarette butt with his DNA on it they would use his DNA to prove that he was there and no amount of surgery, wardrobe, makeup, media adoration and awards, or anything else would make him not the guy who was involved in that wreck. DNA cannot be negated by anything the individual imagines or wishes were true, otherwise Rachel Dolezal and Shawn King would actually be black, Elizabeth Warren would actually be Cherokee, it is your identity to the rest of the world, like it, or not.

As for travel, I've been to at least 26 states and DC, 11 countries on 4 continents, and lived abroad for 2 years. I can say with some confidence that mental illness knows no borders but every place I've been recognizes there are men and women and, had I committed crimes there, they would use DNA evidence against me if they had it.

TB1 to That kid from Kindergarten Cop

Well, if you've done that much travelling, you ain't learned much about the experience of being human from it.

Caitlyn Jenner is exactly the same individual as Bruce Jenner. And the DNA proves it. Big surprise. Rachel Dolezal's DNA is Caucasian. Yeah. Even she would admit that.

I don't know what's up with Shaun King, I suspect he'd deny having much Caucasian dna if he could.

I really can't fathom why you don't get the difference between who someone was born, which they have no control over, and who someone - is - in terms of who they feel like, who they wish to be, who they prefer being, and how they wish to be perceived by others.

Identify as Christian? That is entirely cultural. Or American. Or Canadian. Or British.

Asians born and raised in China don't identify the same way as Asians born and raised in America, even if there is some overlap. Chinese vs. Chinese-American.

So, what if Jenner said she's a male (DNA) woman (subjective identity)? Would you understand that?

That kid from Kindergarten Cop to TB1

It is not difficult to discern what these people are pretending to be. But if I put on a bear costume and start roaring and crapping in the woods, that wouldn't make me really a bear. If I professed myself to be a bear to the world, if I "came out" as a bear, if I cried and threatened to harm myself if you didn't treat me as though I was a bear, that still wouldn't make me really a bear. If you capitulated and complied with my completely unreasonable demands to be treated like a bear, and engaged in arguments with others on behalf of my "transbear identity", I still wouldn't really be a bear. If I took a bunch of sleeping pills and was able to sleep for an entire day, or hired an anesthesiologist to keep me unconscious for longer and afterward told everyone on social media how happy and fulfilled I felt that I had finally "hibernated", I still am not really a bear.

How a person feels on the inside is entirely their experience. The obese women who insist they are "healthy at every size" and wonder why they aren't obsessed over like real models have an entirely subjective, personal, internal sense that is inconsistent with reality. They too are delusional but how they identify is not important to anyone else until they can convince others which is where globs of warm play dough like you come in. To you, and others like you, either you truly don't believe in an objective reality, or you use the post-modernist tactics of undermining reality (it really doesn't matter which), and your ultimate goal is the disintegration of the culture. Honestly, if we can't agree that Bruce Jenner is not a woman, that Rachel Dolezal is not black, that Elizabeth Warren is not Native American, that I am not a bear, where do we begin to have agreement? How can we rationally discuss more important issues if the easy, fundamentals are even contentious?

TB1 to That kid from Kindergarten Cop

Gobs of warm play-dough. That's not bad, far as insults go.

I do wonder, though, what's it like? What's it like believing you are 100% correct about something you have never experienced? From the outside looking in, it seems like a super power. Like one of the X-Men.

You may, in objective reality, be the one human being on the planet who has the ability to solve problems that researchers who spend their entire careers studying can't resolve, all without immersing yourself either in the experience, or in the study of it, or both.

Amazing. Why aren't you rich and famous? Because if you have that talent, for real, you can eliminate the steps even the most brilliant minds to ever walk the face of the earth have had to take to gain insight into their fields. Hard work, research, immersion, risk-taking, sacrifice. Freud, Aristotle, Plato, Einstein, Hawking, Hitchens, they all had to do it.

You, though, you can do what they can't. Be 100% right with minimal effort. Please go public, for you must be recognized for who you are, the living embodiment of what was previously just the realm of myth: a genius blessed with wisdom - unearned wisdom - from day one.

Amazing.

That kid from Kindergarten Cop to TB1

"Sarcasm: the last refuge of modest and chaste-souled people when the privacy of their soul is coarsely and intrusively invaded." - Fyodor Dostoevsky

Firsthand experience does not make anyone an expert on anything, if that were the case, again using your argument, how could you ever accept the possibility that someone could be transgender? How could Bruce possibly know what it means to be a woman? It is fair to say that I have never experienced gender dysphoria, but it is equally fair to say that no man knows what it is like to be a woman. The best firsthand experience a man can bring is that of a dysphoric man, not a woman.

TB1 to That kid from Kindergarten Cop

So you can be knowledgeable without the experience but Jenner can't?

My god you are a f'en loser.

That kid from Kindergarten Cop to TB1

No, what I'm saying is that there is no way a man can know what it means to be a woman, or vice versa, and to pretend otherwise, like you do, is a ridiculous notion.

What's it like to receive an education in logic and reason from someone you hate so much?

A bit about TB2: TB2 is a full-on MTT (Male-To-Trans), he's pre-op but he admits the hormones. He is passionate about his position and will engage in the debate for days on end.

TB2 to That kid from Kindergarten Cop

Often times, trans boys have penisis and trans girls have vaginas. But yes, some people give more credit to what's between a person's ears, rather than what's between their legs. Often, it's people that aren't particularly well endowed in either region who feel so threatened by LGBTQ people.

That kid from Kindergarten Cop to TB2

Not a single word of your above post is factual.

Only a boy can have a penis and only a girl can have a vagina and no, plastic surgery mockeries of the real things don't count. If you disregard what is between your legs with respect to whether you are a boy or a girl then whatever is between your ears deserves no credit. What trannies do by committing interpersonal fraud is wrong. It is not that anyone feels "threatened" it is that you are lying when you misrepresent the truth. You confuse anger with feeling threatened, but then again, anyone who thinks that their genes and associated genitalia have no relation to their status as male or female is no stranger to confusion.

TB2 to That kid from Kindergarten Cop

Genetically, before either male or female genitalia forms in the womb, the tissue is identical on a cellular level either way. The surgery just refashions this tissue.

That kid from Kindergarten Cop to TB2

If you truly believe that, you are confused again. Male genitalia only forms in those fetuses that have the "Y" chromosome, that is a genetic incongruity on a cellular level. They are dermal cells but not identical and "refashioning" them, long after their exit from the womb, and their full development into their natural state of being, into something they never were and is now incongruous with the rest of the body will not make anyone truly satisfied either. That surgical mockery will not make you believe the fantasy, not you, not anyone pathetic enough to engage you physically. It is a poor substitute for the real thing, starting there and emanating outward. "trans" anything is just as counterfeit as $10 Oakley sunglasses or psychos who go out in public wearing military uniforms and medals they never earned. It is a lie.

TB2 to That kid from Kindergarten Cop

Oh, and you are using a straw man fallacy: there aren't really any people who think that genes and genitalia have no relation to biological sex-- that is in fact the definition of biological sex. Gender identity, however, factually defines an aspect of how the brain shapes a person's gender. And I'd say that the brain is a bit more important than what's between a person's legs. Some people may prove to be exceptions to that, however.

That kid from Kindergarten Cop to TB2

Gender identity is a social construct. How can your brain be incapable of complying with a social construct? That would be like saying you "can't wait in a line" or that "standing on chairs is part of who you are", everyone else understands the utility and logic of doing things the right way but your brain makes you incapable? That's not crazy at all?

TB2 to That kid from Kindergarten Cop

My brain is my brain, not a social construct. I was raised by conservatives in a small town, I followed the family tradition of becoming a firefighter, I became more religiously conservative than all of my family and went to church every week for 20 years. I found Jesus and still call him savior. I married and have six children. I have an advanced degree, I'm a published author, and still, none of these experiences resolved the conflict I've had with my gender assigned at birth. I still identify as a political conservative in many ways, yet I am still transgender. So, from my personal experience, my gender identity is an inborn sense of who I am, something that's been with me since I was a very young child. And this is the typical experience for trans people. They are not liberally indoctrinated people who are just joining a progressive movement to threaten red meat, American flags, and the constitution. They are not a communist conspiracy or a product of academic thinking. Like me, they are people, many of whom are more normal in their social conditioning and values than the shrill fear mongering sheeple crowd can understand.

That kid from Kindergarten Cop to TB2

So your brain is your brain, not a social construct? Well that's not at all what I said. But I should know by now that confusion is the word of the day.

Your personal story is of no consequence if you throw it all out in favor of impersonating a woman 24/7. Your gender was not "assigned at birth" like some administrative error occurred from the department of genitalia delivery at the ACME Genitalia Company. Your "Y" chromosome directed your development in utero, your testes grew and developed right alongside your kidneys, your lungs, your spine, and everything else, and is just as much a part of you. The idea that you would take on the affectations, mannerisms, and personality of someone who does not have your genetic makeup is simply insane. It is not significantly different than the girl who blinded herself or others who have amputated working limbs. Just because your particular brand of BIID is so popular right now doesn't make it less insane.

For the record, I don't doubt your insanity, insanity is a very real thing.

As far as the rest of the strawman argument you put forth, the foundation of post-modernism is the institution of chaos. Promoting chaos by "removing the social stigma" of insanity, by promoting and celebrating the things that would quickly kill less robust societies, the post-modernist floods the zone of common sense and understanding of the world in favor of the chaotic. Borders provide framework, ignore them. Laws represent the common man, flaunt them. Marriage represents certainty, undermine it. And now, "Boys have a penis. Girls have a vagina.", that's a bigoted thing to say. All of these things have natural challenges i.e. war over borders, unhealthy marriages, expansion of malum prohibitum laws into areas that are absurd, and insanity, but that doesn't invalidate their utility and to actively promote their demise is an extension of the post-modernist agenda. So, while you may not have the downfall of Western Civilization in mind, those that would elevate and promote your insanity as anything approaching "normal", do.

TB2 to That kid from Kindergarten Cop

Wow, you know everything about me. That's a sign of true delusion, when a person thinks their ideology gives them permission to define everything according to that ideology, including other people. Don't understand people? Just fit them into your conception of who they must be, even if you are completely ignorant of these people. Bravo for your absurd arrogance.

That kid from Kindergarten Cop to TB2

I don't care to know everything about you (not that you didn't try to give me everything). My problem is that I do understand what you are and cannot be influenced by the media to make me believe that your feelings trump objective reality.

TB2 to That kid from Kindergarten Cop

My feelings don't prevent me from accepting objective reality. I am a trans woman, not a biological woman from birth. I am having to undergo physical changes, afforded by modern medical science, to bring my body into alignment with who I am. This will not change my birth gender or genetic code. I accept reality. But it will change a lot (and already has).

You are the one who can't handle reality and the very real transgender people who share the same planet with you. People who can't "handle this truth" usually are misinformed and have their view of things clouded by fearful alt-right rhetoric. Or they have their own deep insecurities about their own sexuality or identity to work out. The fact that they feel threatened by members of the LGBT community is often a strong indicator of their own lack of confidence in who they are.

That kid from Kindergarten Cop to TB2

Your physical changes are surgical and chemically induced and you don't "have to" just because you are insane. Whatever those changes are they still won't make you a woman and there is simply no explanation that will convince me that your destiny was to be a mutilated, over medicated, insane male that pretends to be a woman, that's absurd.

Again, and I guess repetition is needed with confused souls like yours, it is not "feeling threatened" that motivates people to speak out against this political assertion of the insane into everyday life. It is the fact that you would claim it to be absolutely necessary that you misrepresent the fundamental status of your being that angers those who can easily spot the truth. Lying is not the foundation of a civil society, it is an insult to misrepresent and attempt to "fool" people on a daily basis. You can claim it to be some sort of disability that requires you to do this but that doesn't make it less egregious.

TB2 to That kid from Kindergarten Cop

So, simply label those who don't fit your template as insane, so that you can justify negative treatment of such people?

Even if variant gender identities are the product of a mental disorder, as you claim, those in the medical profession continue to support treatment of this condition with gender confirming procedures and medication. The vast majority of transgender people are happy with transition and the efforts to align their physical anatomy and hormones with their gender identity.

Also, the medical profession no longer labels being transgender as a mental disorder. Instead, it is the gender dysphoria, and the distress this causes, that is the disorder. And the treatment is often medical transition where this dysphoria is persistent and severe.

These are the facts that represent the majority of professional care providers in the world. Your opinion is far less important than theirs in directing medical treatment, policy, and rule of law. So, no, I'm not particularly worried about changing your mind. But I am interested in clarifying issues with those who have ears to listen.

That kid from Kindergarten Cop to TB2

The label "insane" applies, but that is not why you are justified to be treated negatively. As I've pointed out, your insistence that you live as a mutilated, hormone-dependent, poor mockery of a woman is an insult to people's intelligence, it is a mockery of real women, and a violation of the social norms that the rest of society uses to conduct our everyday lives. You separate and highlight yourself, nobody else has done this to you.

Appeals to authority are bogus if that authority has proven itself to be political in nature, as the APA has with it's revisions of the DSM. Their opinions, not "facts", as you said, have no more weight on the matter than anyone else's, they gave that up.

TB2 to That kid from Kindergarten Cop

Also, the real deception was to present myself as a typical heteronormative male, when in fact I have always felt so entirely different on the inside.

In fact, even more than transitioning from male to female, I am transitioning from a person who had to hide who she was to a person who can simply and truly be herself. No deception. I don't even plan on going stealth, but instead being an open transgender woman.

That kid from Kindergarten Cop to TB2

You would be deceiving no one by living and presenting yourself as a male, it is after all what you were born as and grew up to be.

Your feelings on the matter are of no consequence. No one makes any assumptions on anyone's feelings about what it is they present themselves to be. No one looks at a doctor in hospital scrubs and cares whether or not he feels like he's made the right career decision. No one looks at a MMA fighter and wonders if they really wouldn't rather be a pastry chef. The fundamental declaration of your membership in the binary on one side or the other is even more basic than hospital scrubs or shorts with ads on them. It means things to people and your misrepresenting that is a violation of public trust.

TB2 to That kid from Kindergarten Cop

And I don't doubt your insanity either, by the way.

TB2 to That kid from Kindergarten Cop

Oh, and your slippery slope fallacies and alarmist rhetoric inspire more chaos than transgender people could ever inspire. You don't have to promote variant gender identities in order to love the people who are trans or something else. That would be the same as saying that asking for people to love disabled people somehow endorses or promotes the downfall of non-disabled people. In fact, the downfall of non disabled people seems more eminent to me if they are unable to love and live alongside those who have disabilities. Again, your are turning people into social-political constructs so you can vilify them and discard their humanity. That's quite lame.

That kid from Kindergarten Cop to TB2

If the disabled people in your analogy insisted they were fully able or "identify as" fully able and insist that the rest of society is wrong for recognizing their various handicaps, you'd have a better point. I have already conceded that your insanity is a real thing and insanity is almost always a debilitating and unfortunate condition. When you start respecting society's rules and stop lying as a foundational facet of your very being, I'll consider reinstating your humanity.

TB2 to That kid from Kindergarten Cop

You are quite amazing-- a figure of some importance, since you can rescind or "reinstate" someone's humanity. And people think I have mental health issues: ha, ha, ha ;)

That kid from Kindergarten Cop to TB2

It is obviously my approval you seek, since you continue to make the case for yourself. When you violate the social contract that over 99.9% of the world abides by it is you who separates from and discards your own humanity, I simply respect your rejection and allow for it's reinstatement when you return to societal norms.

TB2 to That kid from Kindergarten Cop

Actually, I'm writing for a much wider audience in forums like these, trying to help people in general better understand people who are transgender. There are people like you, however, who are so locked in by ideology and so closed in their view of others, that I doubt my example and explanation will have much effect. Yet, there is occasionally a chance at real connection and understanding. And I feel some obligation to lend a dissenting voice to a one sided and sometimes mindless conversation.

That kid from Kindergarten Cop to TB2

I, and I'm sure others here, have no doubt that you suffer your torments (God only knows how crazy you are to mutilate healthy body parts) but that doesn't excuse your insistence that others play along or that they are the problem when they recognize you as a man.

TB2 to That kid from Kindergarten Cop

Hmmm... well, again, I'm not wanting anyone to go along with a deception. I accept that I'm transgender, and that others might recognize me as such. That said, this doesn't mean that others must insist on calling me "he" and "him" and "sir" in a confrontational way, as if my external expression as a woman is completely unacceptable. When my transition is complete, after all, I will be more female than male. To call me "he" at that point is like calling someone who did three rounds of P90X a "fatty" just because they were a fatty before they did all of that exercise. That's just rude and it's totally disrespectful of the person's newly earned and externally fit body. I don't expect anyone to pronounce me a genetic woman, but they would be ignorant of the facts, at the end of my transition, if they didn't accept that I was more female than male. And at the end of the day, are you going to respect me as a human being? Can you give me any credit for the great struggle and sense of peace I've achieved by transitioning? If so, you can call me "she" and by my female first name (all of which will be my legal identity). If not, you are simply being a jerk who refuses to even be in agreement with my legally recognized identity. That puts you on the outs, in terms of social contracts and consideration of a societal norm that is changing to be more accepting of those who are different.

That kid from Kindergarten Cop to TB2

Your status as a victim of your inner torment or as a victor over it is meaningless in the face of your continued misrepresentation of your identity. I've said, repeatedly that your torment is what it is and that it is unfortunate. That still does not excuse your mockery of women and society as a whole.

TB2 to That kid from Kindergarten Cop

Victorious. And certainly not meaningless. It is meaningless to you only because you are delusional enough to believe that your binary, gender conformist, heteronormative identity is the only one that has value or meaning. This simply isn't true. If it were, you wouldn't be so passionately debating your disagreement with my meaningful comments in this forum.

That kid from Kindergarten Cop to TB2

"gender conformist, heteronormative identity"? Man, you are straight out of Tumblr, or reddit or some other such source of word salad nonsense. That is a lot of letters that you used to say "normal" and my normal identity is not the only one with value or meaning, but it is at least honest and sane.

I discuss these things to ensure that you get the truth from somewhere since I'm sure your Tumblr support group is feeding your delusions and reassuring you that you are "beautiful" and to "ignore the haters". They may have no appreciation for honesty or decency but some people still do.

TB2 to That kid from Kindergarten Cop

Defining reality in specific terms helps us better understand reality. To simply ignore parts of that reality by diminishing clear terminology as "word salad," this is simply an ad hominem attack on being articulate. That may work as an argument with the inarticulate and those who lack faculties for critical thought. But it isn't going to win the arguments that matter. I think even Trump will learn that hard lesson in the end.

That kid from Kindergarten Cop to TB2

Brevity is the soul of wit. - William Shakespeare

Why say with one, two syllable word what you can say with 4 words and more syllables than you can imagine? Because "normal" puts it in terms that highlight your position.

TB2 to That kid from Kindergarten Cop

And as far as using the right word for the right thing, Shakespeare is credited with using more new English words than just about anyone. Don't mistake poor syntax and style with a rich vocabulary.

TB2 to That kid from Kindergarten Cop

"The difference between the almost right word and the right word is really a large matter - 'tis the difference between the lightning-bug and the lightning." Mark Twain

TB2 to That kid from Kindergarten Cop

Ah, the righteousness of being normal. You must deserve a medal or something. I'm sure you gloat about being "normal" as your greatest attribute to all your friends, but especially those people who can't be your friends because they are disqualified because of their differences. How awesome are you, Mr. Normal?

That kid from Kindergarten Cop to TB2

Certainly my medal for being normal would pale in comparison to your gold in the "Oppression Olympics", that is until you meet a black, paraplegic, illegal alien, muslim, obese, poverty-stricken tranny, in which case your "gold" quickly reverts to bronze. But here's the thing, none of those other characterizations and identities is inauthentic or deceptive in their identity.

TB2 to That kid from Kindergarten Cop

Not misrepresentation. Straight up representation. No mockery, only respect of my fellow human beings, male, female, gender fluid, non-binary, cisgender, or transgender. I can love and respect all. Although I'm more tempted to mock close minded and judgmental people.

That kid from Kindergarten Cop to TB2

If you had any respect for your fellow man you would not seek to deceive him and if you weren't so rabidly misogynistic you wouldn't reduce what it means to be a woman down to their clothing and mannerisms and believe that you can be one based on your feelings. That's far from "love and respect".

TB2 to That kid from Kindergarten Cop

I don't reduce being a woman down to superficial things. In fact, it's something deeply inherent in who I am that has always made me understand that I always deceived people in presenting and expressing myself as male. Hence, the reason why I know that I am being so much more sincere in being openly a transgender woman. Your conception of trans identity is completely the opposite of what trans people actually feel and are acting upon. You assert judgments about transgender people based on your own poor assumptions and unwillingness to understand anything about them. So your external judgments and opinions are simply inaccurate and unhelpful.

That kid from Kindergarten Cop to TB2

How do you know what it means to be a woman?

Better stated, How could you possibly know what it is to be a woman?

After all, you were never a little girl. When did you get your first menstrual period? When did your boobs grow in? Who was your first boyfriend? Ever have any pregnancy scares in high school? Aren't you scared to death when you have to walk down the street alone and have some creepy guy just start following you knowing that he's a foot taller and 50 pounds heavier and could do great harm to you if he wanted?

All of these things are abstractions to you and I. You have to attempt to imagine how that would make you feel because you never lived these things. The best you can bring to the table is your upbringing as a confused and tormented guy. How can you lay claim to any other identity, especially when you can't possibly know what that identity entails? You are mocking REAL women.

TB2 to That kid from Kindergarten Cop

Actually, I can relate to the worries about walking alone at night, and some experiences of biological women are becoming more and more relatable for me. But yes, I will never experience many things that most biological women experience. Still, it wouldn't be kind or fair to not identify a woman as a woman if she had a hystorectomy or was born with a condition that prevented her reproductive system from functioning or a womb that can't hold a child.

In the end, I would just argue for kindness, understanding, and no fear mongering when it comes to trans people. Most of us do not want to hide or deceive anyone, especially in a day and age when it's now survivable and tolerable to be openly ourselves.

That kid from Kindergarten Cop to TB2

"it wouldn't be kind or fair to not identify a woman as a woman if she had a hystorectomy or was born with a condition that prevented her reproductive system from functioning or a womb that can't hold a child." Nobody ever would, does any of this apply to you though? No? Is it because you are a guy?

TB2 to That kid from Kindergarten Cop

I'm a trans woman. A biological male who is transitioning to a female identity. And no matter how imperfect or puzzling that may seem to others, it will allow me to feel as though I'm at last able to interact and fit into society in a more honest way.

That kid from Kindergarten Cop to TB2

So it's your absolute biological imperative to be "imperfect or puzzling...to others" and there is no other viable recourse for your life? You have the unyielding need to be the subject of children's stares and adult's hushed whispers to each other? The only "honest" way to live your life is as "a potentially maligned minority"? That is you, self-actualized?

TB2 to That kid from Kindergarten Cop

Well, those aren't the outcomes I'm obviously aiming for, but they may be real outcomes none the less. I don't need to pursue being imperfect and puzzling, I just am imperfect and puzzling (even to myself, to some degree). I would rather aim for perfection. But I have to be forgiving toward myself when I am unable to achieve the impossible.

That kid from Kindergarten Cop to TB2

"Impossible", careful, you might have stumbled upon a nugget of truth. You realize that your stated goals in your pursuit to "fit into society in a more honest way" means NOT fitting in to society anymore? You close your circle of understanding and acceptance by diving deeper into the community that is exclusive by its rejection from society AND its rejection of society.

TB2 to That kid from Kindergarten Cop

I think we are now talking about two things, and each are important.

First, there is who I am, which is my individual identity, comprised of genetics, biological sex, natural inclinations, perhaps spiritual character (the soul), socialized or learned behaviors, circumstantial factors (where I was born, to what parents, and into what opportunities), sexual orientation, gender identity, and finally who I become through my own choices and accepted patterns of thought.

Some of these identity traits are obviously developed during interactions with other people and through how they see me.

That's sort of a breakdown of everything that comprises who I am.

Then there is that larger identity that belongs to society itself, which has its norms, its conventions, its laws, its national identity, national and regional leadership, differing political parties, the various sub groups with their differing ethnicities, religious beliefs, job descriptions, regional values, family dynamics, economic statuses, and levels of education.

As far as who I am, as an individual, some of these things were settled at birth, some have developed over time, and some, to varying degrees, I was able to shape myself with my own free will. Some seem to be shaped by societal forces, like a river smoothing a rock. Others seem to spring from the deepest sense of my self, separate from my own conscious will or from the shaping of societal forces. These later characteristics get at what we might conceive as a person's soul, that unchangeable character with which a person is blessed or cursed at birth.

I am blessed to be transgender. And yet I aspire to get along with others in society and to help those in need. I identify as an American, a Christian, and a very lucky father. No one of these completely overrules the other, but in order to pursue happiness and be my best self: my individual efforts do benefit greatly from other members of society accepting and allowing my participation even though I am different and belong to this smaller minority of transgender people.

People who encourage or accept fear, bigotry, and discrimination of transgender people-- they certainly make it more challenging for me to participate fully and richly in society. And their justification for this discrimination is usually an explanation that I've chosen to be a problem for society, that I've chosen to "not fit in."

But for most LGBTQ people, it does feel as if they were born that way. So telling me or someone else in the LGBTQ community to "simply fit in," is like asking a black person to change the color of her skin, or a Jewish person to become Irish.

That kid from Kindergarten Cop to TB2

Not many sane people would consider themselves blessed to be internally obligated to mutilate themselves and imitate the opposite sex for the rest of their lives. In fact, no sane person would.

How does your sex escape the list of immutable circumstances of birth like race and ethnicity?

TB2 to That kid from Kindergarten Cop

You say it doesn't make the list. But I say it does. This is not only an ideological divide between us, but it's an experiential one. I have experienced this sense of being born completely different. Yet, interestingly enough, if someone told you (I assume a heterosexual) to choose to be attracted to the same sex tomorrow, you would refuse, not so much on moral grounds about choices, but on the grounds that you are a heterosexual and have always liked the opposite sex.

That kid from Kindergarten Cop to TB2

There you go attacking my normalcy again.

Homosexuality is an unhealthy and unproductive lifestyle/behavior /orientation. It is not particularly deceptive in its nature through, and requires no real adjustment for other people. When meeting a homosexual, normal people aren't asked to participate in a lie.

When meeting you, so as to avoid being labeled a "bigot" or "fillintheblankophobe", a discerning individual, despite the clear fact that you are not a woman, would be required to act as though you were. So in your world it is rude not to act in a way opposite to the truth. That's not a world that will completely exist outside of your imagination. And to the extent that you will personally experience it, keep in mind that the individuals participating are quick to discard reality and you probably shouldn't do any legal or financial dealings with them.

TB2 to That kid from Kindergarten Cop

I intended no attack on your normalcy. Rather, I simply asked you to consider what it would be like if you were in the shoes of the other person. A request for empathy is not an attack on who you are. Suffice it to say that the trans person feels just as settled in their nature as a heterosexual feels settled in being attracted to the opposite sex, or a homosexual feels settled in being attracted to the same sex. That said, sexual orientation and gender identity are certainly two different parts of what makes a person tick and should not be confused.

Furthermore, I don't expect someone to go along with a lie when they encounter me. I will either pass as a woman or I won't. I don't expect people to lie about this, but we also don't defend confronting ugly people with the truth that we think they are ugly or unattractive. Rather, we can still respectfully call that person sir or ma'am without indicating we want to sleep with them and without lying to that person by saying they are beautiful or handsome.

The standard ettiquette for mannered and compassionate people is to meet others where they are at and show them brotherly or sisterly love.

Any other standard of behavior is not a kind of normalcy that I think is good or would ever support.

That kid from Kindergarten Cop to TB2

You might need to confront ugly people with the truth if they "identify as" a supermodel that day. After all their "aesthetic identity" has nothing to do with their external biological features, these two concepts are completely unrelated. I know this because I read it on Tumblr or reddit or something, and if I didn't read it there, I'll post it there and then it becomes so.

On the encounter bit, let's say you meet someone who is legally blind and they have their suspicions, they let their nice guy self go along with the facade thinking "this tall woman with the husky voice might be a dude, though". He lets it go until he talks to a 3rd party about you and asks, then finds out, how is he supposed feel, having been made a fool of? That's cruel.

TB2 to That kid from Kindergarten Cop

And I wouldn't do that to the blind person. I've actually met many attractive women over the last couple of years, who I've been attracted to, and who initially saw me as an attractive man. And I told these women during our first moments together that I was a trans woman (until recently, I looked nothing of the sort). It wasn't good for any romantic possibilities, but it was the honest thing to do.

As more people become supportive of trans people, the trans people will be all the more open and honest about who they are. It's not loss of attraction that they fear, but outright violence and discrimination.

It's also an odd contradiction that people like you make in your arguments against trans people: on one hand you are angry at their efforts to fool people. But on the other, you assert that they aren't capable of looking and behaving in a way that actually convinces anyone they are women. But if the latter is true, then how can you be angry about any deception, if it is actually as much of a laughable failure as you assert?

Yes, your arguments against trans people simply aren't honest or logical. Rather, they mask deeper insecurities about yourself that you aren't dealing with openly. Go fix yourself.

That kid from Kindergarten Cop to TB2

The encounter with trannies that can't pass is one of the reasons that the entire proposition is so ridiculous. When someone meets you there's immediately a "wink and a nod" toward your insanity so that everyone can agree to lie to each other for a while. It's a bit like talking about Santa or the tooth fairy in front of children, except you are too old for such nonsense.

There are many though, that can pass and when that happens there is the deception. This is the type of deception that can lead to the violence you fear.

Actually, those who are up front about it and attempt no deception are the less offensive of the two. Asking for dishonesty, that you call "understanding", obviously doesn't bother everyone.

What is dishonest or illogical about these arguments? If someone wants to deal in reality and doesn't want to be deceived on something that is potentially as intensely personal as having encounters with the wrong set of genitals, is that illogical? Oh wait, I'm asking questions about honesty and logic to a tranny that thinks I need to fix myself, that's crazy.

TB2 to That kid from Kindergarten Cop

Again, you jump into irrationality. If the biggest fear is the wrong set of gentitals, gender confirmation surgery addresses that. And you are missing my point about transgender people being more open or honest. Probably the only people that really have to worry about feeling misled and having sex with a transgender person are those men who are exploiting broken and hurting people who've turned to sex work out of desperation. And yes, if you are one of those Johns, or are worried you might be, then yes, you need to go fix yourself. You need as much help as the prostitute.

That kid from Kindergarten Cop to TB2

There is nothing irrational about the points I am making. "Gender confirmation surgery"? That's a nice euphemism for "genital mutilation surgery", which is 100% more accurate.

Attempting to marginalize people who are seeking love and companionship as all being "Johns" taking advantage of the mentally ill is just continuation of your disdain for regular people.

TB2 to That kid from Kindergarten Cop

As for my disdain for regular people: this isn't the case for me. Rather, I wonder, in this day and age of greater openness and acceptance, how anyone of sound mind fears that they will accidentally end up deceived by a transgender person and in a physical relationship with that trans person without knowledge of the trans person's unique past? In this sense, the safer and more accepted trans people are, the less anyone has to worry about this.

And it seems, the only people who have a real concern, are those men who sleep around liberally without concern for real relationships in the first place (including Johns who seek out prostitutes). And this might, in many circles, seem "normal" to many men. But accepting that kind of behavior as normal is then part of the problem.

Finally, your description of gender reassignment surgery is not accurate, but certainly is bleated out of the mouth of close minded sheep who have allowed themselves to become mouth pieces for narrow minded and short sighted talking heads in the media. I doubt you have ever looked into the details of the procedure and all that's involved. But it doesn't matter. You've already demonstrated that your opinions will be stagnate and immobile ones-- the kind limited by your own little sphere of existence.

That kid from Kindergarten Cop to TB2

So then it's unreasonable to think that someone who has dreamed of being the opposite sex their whole life might live out that fantasy to its fullest? Hardly. And besides, the only people who might fall prey to the individual doing the deceiving, are "Johns" anyway? And the behavior of "Johns" shouldn't be normal because it's "part of the problem"?

As far as the the "gender confirmation surgery" or "gender reassignment surgery" goes, if gender itself is a social construct how can surgery rectify it? Are there any other social constructs that surgery can fix? But I digress.

I've seen a documentary and read enough about it to know that my description is accurate and there's no amount of name calling that can change that, mostly because the truth is often stagnant and immobile.

TB2 to That kid from Kindergarten Cop

Gender is more than a social construct; it overlaps with and is defined by biology, brain function, hormones, and yes, it even can be altered rather dramatically through physical changes brought to us courtesy of modern medicine. I'm not sure who you are arguing with in your points, but it seems to be a brainless straw man you've made up in your own mind.

Again the facts are as follows: there is biological sex (which is usually the expected binary, but not always), there is gender identity, gender expression, and sexual orientation. People can find themselves on different sides of all of these aspects of individual existence-- different ends of a spectrum for each. There is a lot of diversity (typically less so for biological sex, but there are 1 in 2000 who don't biologically fit male or female at birth, and this is just because of physical differences in the womb). And at the same time, to say that these aren't also interconnected for an individual-- that my sexual orientation is completely separate from my gender identity-- that isn't quite right either.

I understand that simple minded people want reality to be simple. They want the world and the life on it to conform to an easy formula so they don't have to strain their minds beyond the black and white color scheme that makes them feel safe and comfortable, like a child's blanket they pull up to their chin while they suck their thumbs. This isn't so much of a problem until you use your simplemindedness as a justification to belittle or demean others who don't fit that basic formula.

Overall, you seem to be having an argument with your own odd assumptions, with that brainless straw man you've invented. I don't think I'm even part of the conversation at all. Keep pulling your blankie up to your chin and sucking your thumb, and you will continue to learn nothing.

That kid from Kindergarten Cop to TB2

You realize that by admitting biology is a determinant in gender you are breaking with the Tumblr/reddit orthodoxy? And if biology is a determinant, I have to return to the question, how can you, without ANY biological component of a woman, claim that title, even with the "trans" label in front of it?

You continue your indirect appeals to authority by praising 'modern medicine' and 'professional surgeons', etc. with your fantasy of being able to magically turn a penis into a vagina. But I like to keep things simple?

You keep up the ad hominem attacks like "simple minded" and "children" but you can't answer simple questions.

TB2 to That kid from Kindergarten Cop

If you haven't figured out that I'm not a spokesperson for brainless propaganda, you haven't been listening. Of course biology is part of what comprises a person's gender. In fact, that's one of the more compelling areas of research into gender right now-- is how the biology of the brain shapes gender, not just how chromosomes and more obvious sex characteristics define gender in a simple binary. There has been quite a bit of research into the hormonal and neurological aspects of gender, and there is still a lot to learn and discover here, I imagine.

That kid from Kindergarten Cop to TB2

So you stand on potential future research into neurobiological explanations for your insanity and choose to ignore the established scientific markers of gender? Makes sense.

TB2 to That kid from Kindergarten Cop

You are obviously insane and stupid, since you apparently can't even understand the current science on the issue. I doubt I can help you with that. I've tried.

That kid from Kindergarten Cop to TB2

There's that name calling we talked about.

I'm not the one mutilating my body in the pursuit of a goal that is impossible.

I'm not the one hoping for a magical changing of human nature to suddenly embrace that which is clearly unhealthy behavior.

I'm not the one working to deceive my fellow man.

I'm not the one dependent on my fellow man's willingness to play along with my charade in a social setting so as to spare my feelings.

I'm entirely sane, well grounded, educated, and committed to truth and common decency in a civil society. Watching you mock the fairer sex and pretend to be that which you cannot possibly understand is not the sort of game that interests me. It's not the "current science on the issue" that I can't understand, it's the fact that you believe the crap you say here and your feelings actually are science.

TB2 to That kid from Kindergarten Cop

And no, feelings are not science. But studying the brain and the chemical reactions that produce feelings-- science. It's not a tough concept is it, little wall?

That kid from Kindergarten Cop to TB2

It's a science softer than the gray matter it studies.

Regards,

The stagnant, immobile, brick wall of truth

TB2 to That kid from Kindergarten Cop

Ah, name calling. Yes. You had those names coming... finally. I've explained enough, and then I realize I'm talking to a brick wall. Good bye brick wall.

TB2 to That kid from Kindergarten Cop

People who pay prostitutes for sex have issues. It should not be legal in any state, in my opinion.

That kid from Kindergarten Cop to TB2

The hole that is made by inverting the skin of your penis is literally a mutilated and inverted penis. That is all it will ever be. Sorry to be the bearer of bad news. The fact that a "professional surgeon" (or an amateur one like the guy in Colorado for that matter), performs the procedure or if they are proud of it is as meaningless as half the other crap you want to take credit for and attempt to mitigate the disregard for truth you have.

There are not enough words in the English language to explain why waking up every day, taking your hormone pills, putting makeup on your man face, and knowing that that is the closest you will ever get to defeating the inner demon that demands you escape from what you are, is what you always hoped for your life. That inner torment didn't want to be the closest approximation to a woman as you could manage, to make it to the point that you would consider yourself "more woman than man". That inner torment wanted so much more than you will ever manage and that is truly a tragedy that you couldn't silence that little voice that made demands of you that were simply not possible. You were defeated by the insanity and it drove you to extreme measures in a vain pursuit. Your well being was always going to be the greener grass on the other side of the fence and there is no surgery that can fix that (not that your "professional surgeons" mind helping you discover that).

TB2 to That kid from Kindergarten Cop

I've read plenty of autobiographies by trans women who have reached a place in their transition where they are happy with their external changes and are content with where they are at and who they are. I've already begun to feel far more happy with how I look in the mirror and how I feel. So, again, your characterization of trans women is quite misguided. As for escaping, how would embracing transgender identity help anyone escape anything more difficult than being transgender? Let me run away from the difficulty of being me by claiming an identity that makes me a potentially maligned minority and makes it even more difficult being me?

Yeah, that makes sense (add in sarcastic tone).

No. The only thing that makes sense: being honest and whole is far better than being deceitful and split in two. A trans person who tries to live as you want them to live would always be stuck in the latter darkness of deceit and feeling divided or at war with oneself.

As for gender reassignment surgery, the tissue of male privates is identical in cellular structure to the relevant female tissue, and by surgery, a trans female is pretty much indistinguishable from a cis female.

That kid from Kindergarten Cop to TB2

Let me rephrase the question I've posted a few times. Did you always want to be a girl or did you always want to be a poor imitation of a girl? Does your mutilated, inverted penis self lubricate, or bleed, or make babies? Is it attached to ovaries and did it develop in concert with an attractive hip to waist ratio? Are there mammary glands that indicate your ability to mother a child? You're hardly a Venus figure.

TB2 to That kid from Kindergarten Cop

How many pull ups can you do? Do you save people from burning buildings? Can you run a marathon? Have you read classic literature, or do you just watch sitcoms? Have you read the Federalist Papers? Have you read a biography of each of the founding fathers? Have you saved a girlfriend from a knife wielding rapist who was just released from prison?

I don't know. You sure seem hung up on some pretty superficial nonsense. Maybe it's just me, but it's not your biological sex at birth that qualifies you as a real man.

That kid from Kindergarten Cop to TB2

"How many pull ups can you do? Do you save people from burning buildings? Can you run a marathon? Have you read classic literature, or do you just watch sitcoms? Have you read the Federalist Papers? Have you read a biography of each of the founding fathers? Have you saved a girlfriend from a knife wielding rapist who was just released from prison?"

...

How many women have done all of these things?

TB2 to That kid from Kindergarten Cop

I was just throwing out a bunch of deeper things we might base our assessment of character upon.

That kid from Kindergarten Cop to TB2

Those things sound like a guy.

TB2 to That kid from Kindergarten Cop

I don't need to fit any stereotypes. One of my favorite biological female friends loves reading about history, mountain biking, and dressing like a tom boy. She's very comfortable with her feminity too, and I wouldn't tell her she's less of a woman, or more importantly, less of a human for being interested in some things that might more typically interested in men.

Everyone expresses their gender/ masculinity/ or femininity in different ways and to different levels. Some people are more typical and some people are not typical. I like people who show up on all sides of this spectrum, and I have five straight, non gender conflicted siblings who are all different in this way. I love each of them.

That kid from Kindergarten Cop to TB2

"I don't need to fit any stereotypes." says the guy who is undergoing multiple expensive elective surgeries.

TB2 to That kid from Kindergarten Cop

... not to become a stereotype:)

That kid from Kindergarten Cop to TB2

Then what exactly are you trying to fit, if not a stereotype of what represents a woman?

TB2 to That kid from Kindergarten Cop

Do you have a six pack or do you just drink them?

That kid from Kindergarten Cop to TB2

You buying?

TB2 to That kid from Kindergarten Cop

Ha ha ha! Your best response yet. Now I think I'm starting to like you :)

TB2 to That kid from Kindergarten Cop

How well do your sperm swim? Are you more than the pathetic average 5 inches?

That kid from Kindergarten Cop to TB2

So lady-like. Is this the locker room talk the girls volley ball team used in high school? Oh, wait, you don't have any idea.

TB2 to That kid from Kindergarten Cop

I never said I followed Emily Post's Guide to Etiquette. Certain situations call for different forms of response :)

TB2 to That kid from Kindergarten Cop

No, I don't need your approval, but I do intend to be an advocate for laws that protect the safety and basic rights of transgender people. I am an American first, a father, and a believer in Jesus. But I am also transgender and an advocate for the common good, of even minority groups who are often maligned, misunderstood, and at risk of discrimination and bigotry.

That kid from Kindergarten Cop to TB2

The safety and basic rights of crazy people are already provided for. If you identified as a Koala bear or as Napoleon Bonaparte that doesn't mean that society owes you eucalyptus leaves or a standing army trained and ready to invade the whole of Europe.

Whatever other labels you want to apply to yourself, the one that will get you maligned, misunderstood, and at risk for discrimination and bigotry is the one that violates societal norms, the one where you claim it is your biological imperative to live as a mutilated, hormone dependent, mockery of women. Those other labels, generally few people have any issue with.

TB2 to That kid from Kindergarten Cop

This is a false analogy. Any other cliche fallacies you want to throw at me and pretend they are in any way rational? Of course

I'm not arguing that a person can be a different species or a historical figure. These things are physical impossibilities. However, it is very possible for a man or woman to physically transition to the opposite gender, and our society should indeed provide for the basic rights of men, women and non-binary people.

Author's note: This one, I left alone. I can't remember if I had to move on to something in real life or if I just couldn't deal with the stupid of him saying "it is very possible for a man or woman to physically transition to the opposite gender". But either way, he wasn't done...

Separate story, later date same TB2

TB2 to That kid from Kindergarten Cop

Gender identity is part of reality, and the human brain kind of has more determination in a person's identity than what's between their legs. In my humble opinion :)

That kid from Kindergarten Cop to TB2

You're wrong, (TB2), your "gender identity" is an entirely subjective feeling about how you think you should interact with the world, it is not reality.

Reality is the state of the world as it actually exists, not as it may appear or be imagined.

Your body, though surgically and chemically altered, is not actually the body of a woman. That is how you have attempted to make it appear and will never be what you imagined it should be. That is not reality, that is not a convincing appearance, that is your imagination.

TB2 to That kid from Kindergarten Cop

Yes, and so is your sense of who you are. And it's a big part of reality. Yes, the brain is real (at least for some people-- others may have less upstairs, hence their preoccupation with what people have downstairs).

That kid from Kindergarten Cop to TB2

There is no preoccupation with what anyone has downstairs, there is only disbelief when things are "not quite right" in every other area. You should do some reading on "the uncanny valley", it applies to people in your case.

TB2 to That kid from Kindergarten Cop

I usually find that people who can't have compassion for those who are different-- they are the real creeps who seem inhuman.

That kid from Kindergarten Cop to TB2

Believe it or not, I really do pity your mental anguish. It must be a terrible thing to have to endure. But I can't sit idly by and allow those with mental illness to claim special rights.

If your brain is not comfortable in the mens room, that doesn't mean you are allowed in the ladies room, regardless of how you think you should have been born. That's not fair to my family, to have to endure the indignity of having a man watch them do their bathroom business. Even if you are no longer an intact man, it would require you to show them your ax wound to prove it and that does not make the situation better. It's not just the indignation of my family, it's the completely post-modern arbitrary measure of what it even means to count yourself as a "transgender", if an intact man with a beard and Raiders jersey says "I'm a woman today", that's the bar, that's all your people require, a person's say so. That's insane and is just a formula for chaos as simple as the the recipe for chocolate milk.

Your internal torment is not reason enough for the rest of the world to change, you need to conform to the world.

TB2 to That kid from Kindergarten Cop

No. You pretend that pitying someone makes you a kind person. Really, that's just a mask you wear to hide your judgment and condemnation. And being able to go to the bathroom without threats of violence is not a "special right."

Also, what you are saying is equivalent to this: people in wheel chairs want ramps so they can access restaurants and public facilities, but I am going to object to this because I'm not giving those jerks special rights.

Finally, I just want to use the bathrooms that are already there without people making a big deal out of it, and I want them to know that people like me are not a threat.

I just want to get along without threats of intimidation or violence. And I'm even a nice person who goes out of my way to smile at people and say "good morning" or "good afternoon."

That kid from Kindergarten Cop to TB2

I don't pretend that my having pity on the mentally ill means anything at all. You accused me of being a "creep" and that I had no compassion, I just pointed out that having pity for those who suffer inner torment is not beyond me.

People in wheelchairs do not deny my family members their modesty and dignity. You are not the same.

You, as an individual, may not be a threat, but you as a member of a group that includes physical men, are. The fact that you want to be treated differently is the very definition of "special rights".

If you don't want to face "threats of intimidation or violence", might I suggest not appearing to be a perv, whether you truly are or not, it is the appearance that makes all the difference, and stay out of the women's room.

TB2 to That kid from Kindergarten Cop

Oh, and I am a woman. So I'll definitely go into the women's room.

That kid from Kindergarten Cop to TB2

Okay, just make sure you shave really close that morning and don't act surprised if you meet some guy outside the door who doesn't mind punching another guy's lights out for perving on his wife or girlfriend or daughter. You don't belong there.

TB2 to That kid from Kindergarten Cop

That guy will go to jail for assaulting a woman and he'll probably end up paying out of his butt to support me. Good for him. And he better not be trying to touch my legs, no matter how recently I shaved them.

That kid from Kindergarten Cop to TB2

That's likely to depend on where that guy sits on the societal victim strata. Whichever one of you is lower wins.

TB2 to That kid from Kindergarten Cop

Well, if the guy is assaulting me, he is clearly not a victim. Rather, he is a genuine violent threat. And if he is attacking transgender women, then he is likely motivated by religious bigotry and/or fear induced by ignorance. All of this is assuming that the moron can even correctly identify a transgender woman walking out of the bathroom. Just as likely, this creep who pretends to be a man, will assault a cis gendered woman with some masculine traits. Either way, the guy is likely too stupid and too poor in resources to properly defend himself in court. He might go for the insanity plea, and this would actually probably be close to the mark, as only an insane person would assault women coming out of a women's bathroom, and then try to claim that the act was in defense of women.

That kid from Kindergarten Cop to TB2

You really have something against religious people, huh?

It won't be an insane person that attacks you, it will be someone whose girlfriend rats you out, and he may be some roided up MMA fighter that could really do a number on you. That could be the least of your worries depending on what state you play that Russian roulette bathroom game with. For your sake, you'd better be able to pass.

TB2 to That kid from Kindergarten Cop

There are ways that a girl can defend herself. Also: I am a Christian, but I have come to pretty much despise religion and phony people who use ancient text they can't even understand to justify their own hate.

TB2 to That kid from Kindergarten Cop

Oh, and you are truly an idiot :)

A bit about TB3: TB3 is just a garden variety post-modern SJW who thinks his pro LGBTBD position is smarter than the rest of the world.

TB3 to That kid from Kindergarten Cop

Do some research. And if too nuanced for you, try growing that penis.

That kid from Kindergarten Cop to TB3

I read a dozen biology books and they all supported my position. Then I watched a video on (porn website) with your m0+h3r and now doubt is creeping in.

TB3 to That kid from Kindergarten Cop

Grow a brain then read again

That kid from Kindergarten Cop to TB3

What is it that you think I would find? The only place trannies exist is in psychology books. That doesn't make them any different than crazy people. Sure crazy people exist but that's it.

TB3 to That kid from Kindergarten Cop

Re-read. Also OvercomingBigotry101 ... If then you still aren't any wiser, accept that there's no cure for bigotry and stupidity ....

That kid from Kindergarten Cop to TB3

So if I were to abandon reality and embrace fantasies, not my own fantasies, but the fantasies of others, as a new reality, would I then no longer be a "bigot"?

TB3 to That kid from Kindergarten Cop

How about embracing reality and becoming authentic and real about it in your dealings with others. It builds a positive image, develops character, enables learning and enlightenment, builds trusting and meaningful relationships .... in a word 'integrity' or 'authenticity' if you prefer. Go on, try it! I dare you.

That kid from Kindergarten Cop to TB3

How is participating in the fantasies of others, in any way, "embracing reality"? Or "becoming authentic and real" about anything? What about indulging the delusions of the insane "builds a positive image, develops character", etc? What planet are you on?

TB3 to That kid from Kindergarten Cop

Planet REALITY ... deal with it.

That kid from Kindergarten Cop to TB3

"Planet REALITY"? More like "Planet REEEEEEEEE". If you believe men can be women and women can be men based on nothing more than their saying so, there is no "reality" in your life.

TB3 to That kid from Kindergarten Cop

Read. Think. Research. Re-read. Think again. Learn. Grow.

Or accept there's no cure to blissful ignorance and bigotry.

That kid from Kindergarten Cop to TB3

You are free to "Read" (Tumblr). "Think" (use drugs). "Re-read" (Reddit). "Think again" (another bong hit). "Learn" (imagine). "Grow" (your own). All you want and that won't change biology or reality.

I do accept that there is no cure to your blissful ignorance and bigotry.

TB3 to That kid from Kindergarten Cop

What do you know about these people (to name a few)?

Lieutenant Colonel John Laurens

Ian Mathison Turing

Petty Officer Marissa Gaeta

Petty Officer Citalic Snell

General Brigadier Tammy Smith

Technical Sergeant Leonard P. Matlovich, (Vietnam War vet)

Colonel Margarethe Cammermeyer

Johnnie Phelps

Madelynn Taylor

Lt. Dan Choi

Capt. Jim Pietrangelo II

Petty Officer Larry Whitt

Petty Officer Autumn Sandeen

Cadet Mara Boyd

Cpl. Evelyn Thomas

Thea Spyer

US Navy Seal Kristen Beck

Respect!

That kid from Kindergarten Cop to TB3

I know that if they were born with a penis that they were boys and that if they were born with a vagina that they were girls.

TB3 to That kid from Kindergarten Cop

Another reality for you to chew on and digest ... It's not about simply saying 'I don't want my penis / vagina, so I'll change it to a vagina / penis' ... but that is too nuanced for you to get your head around - let alone, simply accept it.

That kid from Kindergarten Cop to TB3

There is nothing about participating in the delusions of others that would make me "authentic" in any way. In fact doing that would throw anything resembling "authentic" out the window. Participating in the delusions of others does not develop character, learning, enlightenment, trust, or meaningful relationships, it would be a relationship established in the mutual agreement to ignore the simplest facts of life, that's insane and essentially the opposite of "integrity" and "authenticity". Is English your second language? Because you have the opposite ideas associated with some pretty basic terms.

A bit about TB4: considers himself quite the geneticist and seems ready to go to the mat to muddy the waters on my statement with a discussion on chromosomes, which is one of the most common responses I get from people when they point out the XX/XY difference as a way to offset surgical mockeries being counted. For the record, surgical mockeries do not count, never have, never will.

Common responder 1 to That kid from Kindergarten Cop

And the people with both are...??

That kid from Kindergarten Cop to Common responder 1

Hermaphrodites.

Common responder 1 to That kid from Kindergarten Cop

Ok...

So we agree there is a third catagory.

Youre wanting to argue about what we call it?

That kid from Kindergarten Cop to Common responder 1

"Boys have a penis. Girls have a vagina." is a movie quote (you can follow the link in my profile to watch the clip). I post it for laughs.

Hermaphrodites that don't require microscopes or MRIs to

diagnose occur in about 1 out of 2000 to 2500 births according to most research. That is a statistical anomaly, not a 3rd gender. In these cases, these people have my pity and best wishes for a life that they find fulfilling and happy. If anyone is entitled to a bit of gender confusion, it's them. If you want to argue about the word "Hermaphrodite" you can but I really don't care what you call them, "hermaphrodite" holds exactly the same meaning as any other term you want to insist that others use.

TB4 to That kid from Kindergarten Cop

Not all combinations of xx yy are Hermaphrodites.

That kid from Kindergarten Cop to TB4

Yeah, well, you have fun deciphering all those. The fraction of a percent of genetic anomalies out there really don't concern me. I know about them because I read a lot but they don't occur often enough to make me concerned about it. I wish these poor souls well. But I think any designation that falls into a convenient, easily determined binary over 99% of the time should probably be listed as a checkbox on govt. forms. If California wants to play to the true hermaphrodites out there and set aside another square half-inch of space on their forms so they can check that box, that's up to them.

TBH, I predicted this would happen a week or two ago, it's not hard to see the crazy train coming down the crazy tracks in California.

TB4 to That kid from Kindergarten Cop

Why is it crazy?

That kid from Kindergarten Cop to TB4

It is a move toward chaos. In the extremely unlikely event of a child born with indeterminate sex (most reports indicate 1 in 2000 to 2500 births), there will likely be a level of development in more one direction than the other, genetic and other tests can be done to investigate further, then if it still can't be decided, you could just leave it blank and come back to it later.

They aren't doing the child any favors by marking their birth certificate as "exclude me" later in life. If the child wants to join T-ball, or boy scouts, or any other sex exclusive activity, many times a birth certificate will be required, not always to determine sex but usually to determine age. At that point you expose the child to potentially uncomfortable discussion by putting whatever organization into a position to have to make decisions that are not spelled out in their directives. Under the "come back later" plan, they would be able to mark whatever sex it is that the child is indicating that they will gravitate toward and not face those hurdles. This is nothing more than seeding the fields for lawsuits at a later date if the organization doesn't pay the lawyer today for preventive measures. So, chaos.

TB4 to That kid from Kindergarten Cop

The six biological karyotype sexes that do not result in death to the fetus are:

X – Roughly 1 in 2,000 to 1 in 5,000 people (Turner's)

XX – Most common form of female

XXY – Roughly 1 in 500 to 1 in 1,000 people (Klinefelter)

XY – Most common form of male

XYY – Roughly 1 out of 1,000 people

XXXY – Roughly 1 in 18,000 to 1 in 50,000 births

That kid from Kindergarten Cop to TB4

And none of these actually result in a condition that would make anyone mark a box other than "male" or "female". Do you have a point?

TB4 to That kid from Kindergarten Cop

Yes, and box marking or not marking is such an important point, isn't it? I suppose it beats having you think.

That kid from Kindergarten Cop to TB4

None of us can "think" our way to a "third gender". None of your genetic mutations listed there invalidates anything I've said. Until you can make a cogent point I am going to assume that you are just a troll.

TB4 to That kid from Kindergarten Cop

Try reading. "Sexing our Bodies"

That kid from Kindergarten Cop to TB4

You can replace every book in the Library of Congress with books just like the one you are talking about and surround it with at least as many doctors as books that say they agree and that still won't create a 3rd gender out of thin air. When the binary works over 99.9% of the time based on a simple visual check, that's what people will go with. You might as well bet on "the edge" every time there is a coin flip and insist that others consider that to be just as viable an option and worthy of discussion before a decision has to be made. There are 2 genders and there are birth defects but something so rare does not warrant elevation to the same status as the 99.9+%. Do we classify conjoined twins as anything other than a birth defect? No, something went wrong with the development. Are kids born with heart defects classified as anything other than having birth defects? No, something went wrong again. Downs syndrome make people not people anymore? Nope, birth defect. Should we start calling midgets, "Hobbits"? See where this is going? Do you want to reclassify and attempt to invalidate perfectly reasonable and useful scientific distinctions based on a birth defect? That's ridiculous.

TB4 to That kid from Kindergarten Cop

Sad to say, but as you seem to be uninterested in dealing with the science presented in "Sexing Our Bodies", and only interested in furthering your own home spun version, I think this conversation is over. Go ahead, have the last word. That's what you want, isn't it?

That kid from Kindergarten Cop to TB4

I'm not interested in your appeal to authority, that's my point. You and plenty more like you have repeatedly noted things like Kleinfelter, and AIS, and whatever other genetic abnormalities are out there to attempt to justify doing away with "the gender binary" and institute a "gender spectrum", that's not going to happen as long as there is an effective visual binary line that is as easily determined as what reality has provided. The rules for society based on that binary are not unreasonable to the 99.9+% of people unaffected by actual hermaphroditism. To the actual hermaphrodites out there, and I've been consistent about this, I would grant you the gender confusion without question. If that's your case, you can read my public profile and see my beef is not with hermaphrodites. How can anyone begrudge the circumstances of another's birth? But at the same time, I'm not willing to give up on polite society and scrap all the rules for the benefit of 0.04% of the population, that's dumb.

A bit about TB5: TB5 is an over the top, sassy intact male and a believer in himself as a woman. Completely self-absorbed and full of himself. One of the most truth averse and stuck in denial believers in the fantasy I've ever encountered.

TB5 to That kid from Kindergarten Cop

Never heard that one before! Your brilliance has changed me *sacrasim*

That kid from Kindergarten Cop to TB5

Glad I could help. *sarcasm* (not "sacrasim")

TB5 to That kid from Kindergarten Cop

The only thing you helped is your own hate.

That kid from Kindergarten Cop to TB5

I'm in far less danger of killing myself than people with your particular brand of mental illness, so who is the one with all the hate? You hate yourself far more than I ever could.

TB5 to That kid from Kindergarten Cop

This same stupid argument again. 80% of trans people report violence and sexual harrasment. The suicide rates are because of the constant harassment from people like you.

I love myself. I'm happy. It is you who are dictating to me my own condition. That is hate and discrimination. You have no right to tell me who or what I am.

That kid from Kindergarten Cop to TB5

Trannies report such high rates of violence and harassment because they are insulting people's intelligence by their deceptive behavior, the more convincing the deception, the deeper the insult. They also run higher rates of histrionic personality disorders and that usually leads to running into a less wholesome element anyway. As for the "constant harassment" you feel, well that's called your conscience and it comes from inside, the fact that it leads to higher suicide rates is just an indication of the malignant nature of the delusions and compulsions.

You don't truly love yourself, you can say it a million times but that doesn't make it so. You hate yourself so much that becoming the polar opposite of what your genetics dictate appears to be the best option you can fathom. And your hate is so virulent that you have extended it to others who resemble what you hated picturing yourself as.

And one more thing, I have every right to tell you that you do not qualify as a woman in any sense of the word. You lack the body, the experience, and the expectations that goes with being a woman. You are a masquerading and pretending fool that the rest of the world just tolerates for the sake of expediency.

TB5 to That kid from Kindergarten Cop

And you know this how? You know what I am, how? Do you have (the required to legally transition) psychiatric degree my therapist does? Do you have the medical degree my (also required) doctor does? Are you me? Do you have a clue what or who I am, why I am this way?

Simply because you decided, what you wish to hear you know more about the situation than I? You must be an expert. You are an expert on the transgender community? You are so well educated in the situation you can dictate something you know nothing about personally?

Have you ever talked to a doctor or a psychiatric professional about who I am?

But you know, how? Reading rightwing propaganda sites? Having an opinion? Because you don't like me, or what I am, you know better than I? I "hate" myself because you decided?

You know my body? You know my experiences? You know why I did this? I'm just to stupid and a dumb creature because you are a gender expert? I just hate myself? So I'll happy live the rest of my life this way, but you know what I am? Have you ever met ONE trans-woman?

It's easy to call someone a true monster. It's easy to judge. Just because you're not me. You think I wanted this? It would have been infinitely easier to have been born like you. I wasn't. I simply am what I am. You can quote contorted junk all you like. That still doesn't mean I don't know who I am, or be happy as that.

I defend myself because I am strong enough to. Why are you here attacking people you actually know nothing about?

That kid from Kindergarten Cop to TB5

Your "personal experience" qualifies you as an expert in delusional thinking. If you were born with a penis, you are a male. There's no changing that. There's no therapist, no surgeon, no witch of any cardinal direction, nor magical wizard of some far away land that will make you the opposite sex.

I know plenty about reality. You don't live with the benefit of having embraced reality in a while so how can you speak on it? What do you know about reality? Do you have a degree in reality like the rest of the world? Have you ever talked to someone who is actually a man or a woman? You think you get to decide what a woman is, when you aren't one personally? How do you know, because you hate yourself? See how tiring that line of BS is? And no I've never met a "trans-woman" because there's no such thing. There are play-acting, delusional fools like yourself who have mutilated themselves and/or overdosed on female sex hormones but that doesn't qualify them as anything other than eunuchs or science experiments. Your happiness as a eunuch/science experiment doesn't confer any more legitimacy toward your claim of being a woman than wearing pretty dresses or growing out your hair. Nothing can be done to make reality stop being so.

Yes, yes, you're a precious snowflake victim of your own psychosis who would have had it easier if you were just normal but the victim narrative fetish just felt right for you, huh? I really don't care how you lead your life just don't lie in the public square and dare people to call you on it for fear of being thought insensitive because you will get, apparently unwelcome, reminders of reality from those of us who still value the truth.

TB5 to That kid from Kindergarten Cop

Oh bunny-foo-fo, is that a trigger? You upset at the big bad evil tranny? Do I make you nervous? Afraid you want me? Or worse, respect me?

Trying asking for credentials, experience or education? Is that a problem for you? Big Truth Man!

Poor big truth man, I, who you don't know put on a dress and dared to flip off the world to be true being. Poor you. It must be so hard for you to have human decency.

Do I sound like a f'n victim boy? Do I sound like a man to you? Do you think I am here for s & giggles. For your amusement?

I won't let my child grow up in a world here he can't be himself.

Welcome to what being a female is.

Foo-fo.

That kid from Kindergarten Cop to TB5

What in the world do you think you have said here that would be worthy of respect? What do you think would be attractive about you?

I have plenty of education and more importantly I bring objective, measurable, truth to the argument.

Your word selection, challenging tone, and name calling are certainly not very ladylike. You type like someone angry at life, daring all who you encounter to challenge your lies while promising more cry-bullying to make them seem like heartless jerks. Well, BFD.

Your child, sad as that prospect is, will have every opportunity to achieve whatever he wants in life; whether it be astronaut, cancer researcher, even a Republican, but he can never be a girl.

You have no idea what being a female is.

TB5 to That kid from Kindergarten Cop

You have no idea what being a man is. Or a gentlemen.

There's my picture. My name, who I am? I'm hot. And I know it. Because I actually do love myself meanie.

What you really want is an intellectual woman to kiss your gross hairy behind and call you master.

Because you have no idea what being a man is.

That kid from Kindergarten Cop to TB5

You'll have to excuse me if I immediately discount whatever opinions on what being a gentleman, or any other type of man, that come from someone who can't figure out what he is.

As far as getting an intellectual woman to kiss my behind, do you know any?

TB5 to That kid from Kindergarten Cop

Yes, I know plenty. Except they aren't into being repulsed. Or vomiting.

This is all ladies club.

That kid from Kindergarten Cop to TB5

Well, not ALL ladies.

TB5 to That kid from Kindergarten Cop

Total jerk bigot hater is not high on a girls priority list.

That kid from Kindergarten Cop to TB5

Again, you have no idea what is high on a girl's priority list.

TB5 to That kid from Kindergarten Cop

It's funny cause you think that. But you have NO idea. Lol. Of only you or any of these haters knew the truth.

I will tell you this: it ain't you sweetie.

That kid from Kindergarten Cop to TB5

I know as much about what women are thinking as you do.

TB5 to That kid from Kindergarten Cop

Lmfao. Funniest thing ever lol.

Looks down at breasts, cute dress, yoga pants, pretty nails, F on my drivers license, female roommate and sexy body..... Hmmmm. Estrogen, PMS..... Hit on by creepy dudes, rape threats, woman's restrooms, guys stating at your chest, guys always trying to act superior, that thing were other woman disarm there defenses around you because we're all woman and know how actual men are. I won't even go into sex lol.

No dude, as an actual woman, with an actual female mind. You have no freakin' idea. Lmfao.

That kid from Kindergarten Cop to TB5

So fake boobs, how you dress, government documents, a roommate, self esteem, pharmaceutical estrogen, phantom psychosomatic "PMS", associating with perverts, going into the wrong restrooms, and being rightly considered a eunuch by women is all there is to it?

You are every bit as far away from being an actual woman today as you were the day you were born. You have a male body, a delusional male mind, and no freakin' idea what a real woman thinks and feels.

TB5 to That kid from Kindergarten Cop

I grew the boobs myself. There all real. I have fabulous style. Woman don't live with men, just women. We walk around naked and share clothes too. It's the exact same estrogen that cis-women are prescribed. For everything from menopause to hysterectomys. Actually PMS from the actual estrogens. Hormones still work that way, my roommate and I even synced up. The legal name and gender marker change require approval from both a medical and psyciatric proffesional. Did you know boob sweat is everybit as bad as jock sweat. Lol. I live, all day everyday as a woman. In every way. You are simply a fool.

I don't know what is is with you haters. Despite what all of science and medicine say, which I've actually lived. You all cling so hard to your silly belief it's impossible to have the brain of one gender the born body of another. Really it's not that complicated. It's simple biology. I'm sorry it's so earth shattering to you to have to realize I exist. You have never even met one of us. What exactly makes you all know better than I what I am? There's nothing man about me. Nothing about the way I live. Nothing man about how I am.... But you'll really still tell me and my soft long hair, silky skin, full body multiple orgasms even, that my everyday as a woman is fake? That's just stick your fingers in your ears and go lalala silly.

You little man couldn't even begin to imagine the reality of it. The truth.

"Real" women who meet me all know. They can instantly tell. All girls can. All your hate and fake politics are simply afraid of the truth. Honestly I think you all just watch trans porn and are ashamed of it. Which no one should be of course.

You can tell me about myself all day long, but you will still just be an ignorant small minded little man, who probably can't get laid.

That kid from Kindergarten Cop to TB5

Let me break down every lie just posted in your opening paragraph.

You have medically induced gynecomastia, they're the result of your science experiment and not natural.

Your opinion of your style is just an opinion and completely irrelevant in supporting your claims to be something you can never be.

I have lived with my wife for several years now so, like billions of others, men and women can and do live together. Yes we walk around naked and she will throw on my dress shirts from the office and she looks sexy when she does.

The estrogen you inject is not replacing what your body used to make, it is foreign to your body and is countered by the adult levels testosterone that your body naturally made for all those years.

If you are born a male, you cannot have menopause, a

hysterectomy, PMS, or any cycle to sync with anyone. Further evidence of your delusions.

A legal name change is easy and depending on the state, the marker of male or female can be simple too. In Canada it can be done all before lunch, without any proof at all.

You probably do have experience with jock sweat so that's the only truth of the paragraph.

You PRETEND all day, every day, to be a woman.

There's the truth and even a fool can deliver the truth.

It's not hate for you, people who are suffering from mental illness are to be pitied, treated, and helped to return to reality. All of medicine has an obligation to keep you healthy and if that means indulging your fantasies to prevent you from killing yourself, then they have at least bought time to continue to study your case. The expediency of accommodating you is just as water flows down hill, it's the path of least resistance, but you still can never be a woman. Your commitment to your delusions doesn't change reality though. People will eventually capitulate to your arguments because they tire of your insistence, threats, and name calling, and call you a woman, but nobody, including yourself, truly believes it because you lack the equipment necessary to meet the most basic requirements of being a woman. You are a man.

TB5 to That kid from Kindergarten Cop

You are just one politically motivated talking point after another, aren't you honey. Did I hit a nerve?

Today's Transgender Day of Remembrance for those of us who were murdered, in cold blood, by men like you.

You realize your entire argument is an invented, ideological fake talking point right?

Your inability to think for yourself is sorta astounding.

Gynecomastia? Really? Talk about stretching. Really? OK, whatever. I have actual female breasts. Not your fat lazy man tits.

I grew, pretty, natural, no surgery breasts. Not gross man boobs. Nice big nipples, they lactate. Tingle in orgasm. Oh honey, you are becoming ridiculous. Your the one with self hate. Is it that you repress wanting us, or being us?

My style, no man could ever replicate.

I was married to a woman for 12 years. DUUHHHH Married couples do that. I plainly said my female non relationship roommate. Roommate. I knew you'd say something stupid like this. Because that's about as far as your intellect appears to go. Of course as an ACTUAL MAN you'd completely utterly fail to see the point. Single women, do not live with "delusional men" or men in general as roommates. But I should have known that point would have flown over your head. Since you don't know how women think. Single women don't run around naked with men in a non sexual way. Did you really never see that point? No of course not you're a man. Why would you not be utterly moronic.

And then, you really go on this ridiculous rant about hormones! Like you have some small clue what your talking about, because your an doctor now! My Balls don't produce testosterone anymore idiot. I went through FULL female puberty. Try that as an adult. Go ahead. Try that one.

For years! That's where the breast comes from. Also all the muscle mass disappears, I developed hips, a butt, smooth skin and hair that grows like crazy. Soft smooth hair. Body hair disappears. Facial features soften. My "junk" became tiny and useless (like a c***)

I could even describe to someone as full of it as you what all this feels like to your body or mind.

You realize everything you said was utter and complete lies by the political ideology you ascribe to.

I PMS because I only have estrogen in my body idiot. That cycles just like in a cis woman, that's why we sync. Of course I have to describe this to a foolish simple man. But that's what estrogen does, whether you believe it or not.

And no, about the legal paperwork. You have no idea what you are talking about. I have a couple Canadian Trans friends actually, who want to come here because it's stupidly hard, and long, and a ridiculous process period. It takes years and years, money, therapy and an immense amount of work. Pain and suffering. If you think this is easy, or fun, or for delusions, you are sorely mistaken. Before Lunch? If you mean years, if at all.

I pretend? You pretend. I already finished my battle.

Since it's Trans Day of Remembrance for my murdered sisters. I'll lay it out real.

You and all the scum posting on here and arguing with me, are the delusional ones. You ate the one hiding a honest truth from yourself.

I'm not living a lie anymore. I've put in my heartache, abuse suffering and pain.

I am real, true, free, happy. It is you who needs to stop lying to yourself.

I'm stronger than you could even imagine. You go ahead and loath the truth.

I'm gonna go be sexy, as hell.

That kid from Kindergarten Cop to TB5

"You realize your entire argument is an invented, ideological fake talking point right?" oh, the irony.

Facts are only talking points if you are engaged in a serious discussion. You are either an incredibly dense true-to-life tranny, or a performance artist troll whose audience is too small, medium too limited, and satire too subtle.

Transgender Day of Remembrance? Is that the day you try to remember what you were like before you went bat guano crazy?

Women can live with whomever they choose to, the fact that you believe you are a woman just makes you the highest grade of non -threatening discussion fodder for her friends.

YouTube search "Lauren Southern sex change" she does EXACTLY what I said could be done before lunch, not waiting a day or suffering at all. Your lies are plentiful and passionate though.

You are a high functioning insane person but you are not and can never be a woman.

TB5 to That kid from Kindergarten Cop

"Folks don't see this. I am the most famous trans woman in Canada. Cops at my door would be national media"

-- My Canadian friend.

TB5 to That kid from Kindergarten Cop

You, boy have so little idea. I didn't not walk into the snake pit of hate after the election of hate against my kind because it was fun for me. I didn't become the most ridiculed, harassed, insulted, attacked creature on earth because it was fun for me.

My blog is listed on my (website). 25 trans women were violently murdered this year. That's only the visually out ones. 90% were women of color. Yesterday was Transgender day of Remembrance. Look it up. My sisters know. They all cared. Because they know what true hate and evil is.

The "mental illness" talking point was around long long before trans people gained public acknowledgment. The same line was used against all homosexuality for decades. Now Milo is a Breitbart idol, and that's forgotten, and the same tired lies are leveled at me.

Men don't get this little concept that straight women don't have straight male roommates because of their sex drives. We don't feel safe around them. We certainly don't act like we do around other women.

Thank you for at least calling me her.

I watched your ridiculous fake YouTube. I went through this process. I also have three trans friends currently living and transitioned in Canada. It took me 2 years of therapy and having incredibly powerful, credentialed doctor, a lawyer and a judge in the most trans friendly state in existence to do all I have.

I carry my paperwork with me everywhere.

You are a tool of your ideology's hate if you believe that garbage. That's the stupidest attempt at journalism I've ever seen. It was obviously staged. Stupidly staged. They don't even use any of the proper medical terminology. Most trans people aren't even recognized because it's so hard to get proper medical help. It is completely impossible to change your gender marker without actually transitioning and both a medical doctor and psychiatric doctors approval, than you go to court!

The truth is, like I told you, and Milo, and all of Breitbart, again and again, is you like all who actually meet me, or us, is we are exactly what we say we are. I am a women. I didn't ask to be attacked by the likes of you. I simply am what I am.

I am not "high functioning" like I'm some sort of addict. I am a proud, strong, good, true, honest woman telling my story so others, myself, don't have to suffer at the hands of haters.

I told you, people meet me, us, they clearly see the truth. Even you can see I am not insane, or a monster, or whatever else the crazies print.

I am simply an actual woman. A smart woman. A proud woman. A good woman. Your politics of hate can kiss my purdy behind, because you want to believe them. You don't want to know the truth. I am obviously what I say.

If facts and truth are what you claim to believe, start believing them. Again, that's my picture, that's my real name. I'm not here to play some game on haters. I'm here to standup for my friends.

I am here to be the Woman I am in my country. My America. I went through hell, I can be respected and not have to put up with this crud. For my sons sake if not mine.

That kid from Kindergarten Cop to TB5

You have a histrionic personality disorder and a Jesus complex.

Chances are that your friends were murdered because they raped someone.

The mental illness argument is valid. Homosexuality is a mental disorder if it causes the individual great distress but there are large enough communities for them to be a part of so that the distress is minimized or they can decide that other people's opinions are meaningless and they can live stress free. Milo and homosexuals in general are doing sex wrong but they would only be delusional if they believed that babies would result. Trannies are delusional. Trannies "believe" that they are what biology plainly shows that they are not. That's delusional.

Women do have straight male roommates, maybe you aren't straight but otherwise it's absolutely possible and probably more prevalent than trannies.

Actual women don't carry around "their paperwork" with them because they aren't trying to deceive anyone and need a doctor's note to not be suspicious.

You are simply a delusional man. A proud delusional man. But never a woman.

Facts are not just what you believe. Can't believe I just typed that and I know it's completely wasted on you.

I'll never respect someone delusional and proud of it. Mental illness is no more a badge of honor than someone proud to have tuberculosis, at least the tuberculosis sufferer would have the good sense to seek out a doctor.

A final word…

I want to thank those that support me in my endeavors to bring truth to the world. There are numerous other issues facing the world that may be more important but this one speaks to me in its absolute absurdity. I do believe that these people believe they are what they say they are but that still doesn't make it real and that's what I will continue to hammer. If atheists attack relentlessly those who are believers in the unknowable, I can relentlessly attack believers in that which is knowable. I will keep up the good fight and look for my fellow travelers to keep posting their opinions on this and many other issues. If you see me out there, keep sending me the good vibes and I'll keep sending you the same.

ABOUT THE AUTHOR

That kid from Kindergarten Cop's dad is a gynecologist. He looks at vaginas all day long.

www.ingramcontent.com/pod-product-compliance
Lightning Source LLC
Chambersburg PA
CBHW071209280526
45787CB00002B/625